KT-539-493

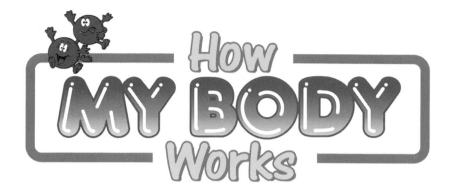

How
MY BODY
Works

The
Environment

Environment In Danger

Town or country?

Have you ever noticed that people who live in towns always love going to the countryside? Why do you think this is? Aren't they happy living in towns?

Big towns and cities have a lot to offer – you can go to the cinema or the theatre, there are many shops and markets and lots of people work in towns. But towns are also often noisy and dirty. People tend to rush everywhere and may be under a lot of stress. That's why they like to go into the countryside to relax.

In the countryside, the air is fresh. The only noises you hear are the twittering of birds and the splashing of water in little streams. And the only dirt you see is mud or cowpats in a field.

The place where we live and the surrounding area is called our **environment**. Even in ancient times people knew that it mattered where you lived. Your environment can make you feel well or ill. People who live in towns do not live in their natural environment. Some people may even become ill because they cannot adjust to life in a town.

Big towns are full of car and lorry exhaust fumes, smoke from chimneys and factory litter. No wonder some people like to spend their free time in the countryside.

HEAVY LOAD

20 Km.   20 Km.

The Professor directs the body's defence system. He and Metro, his lieutenant, work to protect your body. Globus and his team of red blood cells need protection as they travel the body delivering oxygen. So Captain Courageous, chief of the white corpuscles and his friends Ace and Corpo cruise around the body attacking their enemies Virulus, the virus and Toxicus, the bacterium.

VIRULUS

GLOBUS

PLASMUS

GLOBINA

CONTENTS

A new problem?

Living in a dirty environment is not a new problem. People had to live with dirt a long time before the first factories were built. Drinking dirty water made hundreds and thousands of people ill. When many people suffer from a disease at the same time, it is called an **epidemic**.

Hundreds of years ago, the streets were full of rubbish and there were no water taps or toilets inside houses. Rats ran around in the streets and carried diseases from one person to another.

Today our problems are different. We have built large factories to make industrial and chemical products. They use up enormous amounts of energy and give out waste substances – they pollute our planet. This pollution has become so bad that our whole planet is now in danger.

Luckily, humans are intelligent. We understand how much harm we are doing to our environment, so we can try to stop it before it is too late.

When you are in the countryside it is easy to forget that pollution exists. But if you look carefully, you will see that nature is at risk. Every year more and more of the countryside is spoiled as it makes way for towns, roads and factories. Hedgerows and trees are disappearing.

Life on Earth

You can find all sorts of life on our planet – people, animals and plants. There are living things in the sea, on land, on very high mountains and even up in the air. The part of the earth's surface and the air around it in which this life is found is called the **biosphere**.

The air part of the biosphere is a layer of gases called the **atmosphere**. This envelopes the Earth and creates a good environment for humans, plants and other animals to live in. We developed here because everything was just right for us to survive – temperature, moisture, air pressure and light. The balance of these conditions is very important.

When the balance changes we may become ill if we don't adapt quickly enough. When the temperature gets suddenly colder at the beginning of winter we might catch a cold, for example. When it is very warm and moist,

The biosphere is the natural environment for humans. We share it with animals and other creatures. We all depend on each other, just as each link in a chain needs the one next to it.

bacteria thrive and can spread diseases. All plants and animals have to adapt to their surroundings. When we are in hot, moist climates we have to be careful to avoid diseases. If we do not adapt to the change we might become weak towards invading bacteria.

The air in which we live, the atmosphere, is part of our biosphere. It is wrapped around planet Earth like the peel around an orange. It stretches up to a height of 16 km.

16 km

Something's in the air

Every day you breathe in 12,000 litres of air. With so much of it going through your lungs, it needs to be good quality.

Even in ancient times people knew that it was not good to breathe in dirty air. They could sometimes smell danger in the air such as when a volcano had erupted and had thrown out millions of dust particles. They also noticed that smoke from burning torches and fires was not good to breathe in. However when chimneys and air vents didn't exist it was difficult to do anything about it.

Today we know exactly what should be in a breath of fresh air. As you can see in the list, it needs to have the right amount of nitrogen, oxygen, argon, carbon dioxide and small amounts of other gases.

Often there are other substances in the air which don't belong there. That's when we say the air is 'polluted'. Different countries try out different ways to make their air fresh and clean again. They all know that polluted air is not good for people, animals or plants.

Nitrogen	78.09 %
Oxygen	20.89 %
Argon	0.93 %
Carbon dioxide	0.03 %
Other gases	0.06 %

Machines and factories have polluted the air all over our planet. In some areas it is particularly bad – like New York.

If we don't stop this pollution very soon, it will become so bad that we will become ill when we breathe the air.

In the Western world we know that we need to protect our environment. In most countries, governments try to stop pollution. In Great Britain the government is making moves to reduce the spread of towns, and the attack on the countryside and natural environment – you have to get permission to put up new buildings. There are special 'Green Ministers' whose job it is to help stop pollution. Councils provide recycling banks in each town – for paper, bottles and cans. Shops are now selling fewer spray cans that contain harmful gases that damage the ozone layer. All petrol companies now sell lead-free petrol which means cleaner air and less pollution.

KILLER SMOG

London has always been famous. Tourists enjoy sightseeing trips to Buckingham Palace, the Tower, the Houses of Parliament and Piccadilly Circus. Some years ago, London was also well known for something much less pleasant – smog, a horrible mixture of smoke and fog.

In 1952 the smog was particularly thick. People called it a 'pea-souper' because it was as thick as pea soup. But smog is no laughing matter – within only five days more than 4,000 people died from breathing problems. It was time to do something about the polluted air.

A new law made London a smoke-free zone. It was forbidden to use ordinary coal, which makes dangerous smoke, for burning. If anyone burned coal, they had to use a new, smokeless coal. People also built higher chimneys on factories so that dirty air would go higher up into the atmosphere.

With these new regulations, the air in London became better. Today, London no longer suffers from smog. But now they have a new problem to control – the exhaust fumes from millions of cars.

Who is to blame?

Polluted air is not only dangerous for humans, but also for most animals and plants. Air is **polluted** if it contains a poison or if it does not have the right amount of each of its natural parts. Either way, polluted air is dangerous air which may poison the environment. To stop air being polluted, we need to know what makes it so dirty. There are several reasons:

1 Air gets dirty from smoke. Smoke is made when things burn – you can see smoke from bonfires in the garden and wood or coal burning in a fireplace. Our electric and gas heating also makes smoke, but we cannot see it so easily.

2 Industrial sites and factories make an enormous amount of smoke. Some industries, such as foundries and power stations, need to burn material every day.

3 Cars cause a lot of pollution, especially in busy cities like New York and London where there are a lot of cars and people. In New York, for example, more than half the dirt in the air comes from car exhaust fumes.

People can change this – by walking if they don't need to go far, instead of driving. They can use unleaded petrol and they can add catalytic converters to their car exhausts to filter the air. They can also stop racing around – the faster someone drives, the more dangerous the fumes are that come out of the exhaust. It is better to ride a bike or use public transport whenever possible.

4 Burning rubbish makes a lot of dangerous smoke. There are new safe ways of getting rid of rubbish, but not every country uses these. It is best to make less rubbish and to recycle.

Thousands and thousands of tons of dust particles and dangerous gases get into our atmosphere every day. They turn fresh air into a dirty, dangerous mixture.

The top polluters

Which are the most dangerous substances that pollute our air? Where do they come from?

Why do we carry on making them? This chart shows the worst baddies. You see how difficult it is to stop pollution when so many everyday actions harm the planet.

POLLUTER	WHERE IT COMES FROM	
Carbon dioxide	Heating in homes and industrial sites	
Carbon monoxide	Cars, iron foundries and oil refineries	
Sulphur oxide	Combustion engines, aeroplanes, burning rubbish, using fertilisers, forest fires	
Phosphates	Using too many cleaning materials and fertilisers	

Quicksilver	Battery factories, electricity generators, paint and varnish factories, paper making factories	
Lead	Chemical industries, insecticides and sprays	
Oil	Refineries and oil rigs	
Pesticides	Special substances sprayed or spread on the ground to stop pests	
Radioactivity	Nuclear testing, nuclear reactors, ships and submarines using nuclear power	

Why Is Pollution Dangerous?

Take a deep breath

Your lungs make sure that the air you breathe gets into your blood. This is how it happens.

You breathe in through your nose or mouth. The air moves into your bronchial tubes, which are branches of your windpipe that go into the lungs. On its way down it gets filtered, cleaned and warmed up, especially in winter. Moisture is added to it. In fact, you breathe out about a litre of water with the air every day!

The bronchial tree has a fantastic network of little branches called **bronchioles**. These branches make sure that the air gets to the corners of your lungs, which are called **alveoli**.

The lung vesicles in both your right and left lung are where friends meet. It is here that the oxygen in the air meets the haemoglobin in your blood. The two get on really well. They join up, and the haemoglobin takes the oxygen like a piggy-back to all your cells.

The body fights back

When you breathe in dirty air all sorts of ghastly things get up your nose! Luckily, your body has many ways to protect you.

The first barrier for dirty air is your sense of smell. If you got a whiff of smelly socks or a stink bomb, what would you do? You'd probably hold your nose, shout and run away if you had any sense.

The next barrier is provided by all the little hairs and the mucus inside your nose. The mucus traps the bigger particles in the air, such as dust. The little hairs which are called **cilia** move like waves and push the mucus and dust away down the throat. The upper part of your bronchi also has these helpful hairs. When the dust particles trigger these hairs, it makes you sneeze and whoosh! Out goes the dust.

Finally, dirty air comes up against your lungs which act as barriers. They have an army of special phagocytes which are ready and waiting to catch and guzzle up many of the dirty invaders. **Phagocytes** are white blood-corpuscles that swallow bacteria and other harmful invaders.

If you could see all the dirt you breathe in, piled up in one big heap, you would be shocked. Thanks to your body's good defences, most of this filth does not make you ill. As you can see here, if the bacteria like Virulus and his microscopic mates tickle the hairs in your nose, they are all whooshed out in a big sneeze!

Attack of the poison particles

Your body has a number of good defences but some poisonous particles will still manage to get in. The successful invaders usually don't smell of anything – otherwise you wouldn't breathe them in, in the first place. They are dangerous because they attack your cells, poisoning your body and making you ill.

Bit by bit the poisonous particles invade your whole body. You could get very ill. Some parts of your body might stop working altogether. The poison also makes your body weaker so that it cannot fight off bacteria and other invaders.

Stop the poison!

Your cells make endless batches of proteins to cope with all the poison. The proteins are special enzymes which make poison harmless.

Afterwards, round sacs containing powerful enzymes called **lysosomes** come to clean up and get rid of the last few poisons. They cart them away in your blood, down to the kidneys. Finally, all the poison is washed out of your body in your urine when you next go to the toilet.

Here is the inside of a cell. The three little protein chaps are rushing around with their spanners to take a couple of poisonous molecules apart. Two of them have won the battle – their molecule has become harmless. The third one seems to have fainted – obviously his poisonous molecule was too big for him to handle.

Fatal attraction

Carbon monoxide, also known as CO, is one of the most dangerous poison invaders. Together with oxygen, it waits in your lungs for the arrival of haemoglobin, which is an iron-based substance that gives blood a dark red colouring. As soon as the three of them meet, the CO jumps on to the haemoglobin's back, forcing it to drop the oxygen and gallop away.

When the poor haemoglobin gets to your cells, it has no oxygen to feed them. Worse than that – it can't even get rid of the CO which clings on and won't let go. This is not very good for the cells which are hungry for some oxygen.

Scientists have measured how dangerous a CO attack is for humans. When there is only one quarter of a millilitre of CO in a litre of air, we'll suffer from a terrible headache. But if there was one whole millilitre of CO in a litre of air, we'd drop down dead!

Globus is helpless! He had to drop all his oxygen when the carbon monoxide jumped on his back. He doesn't know how to get rid of his heavy load.

However, there is one way to help him. The person in which he lives needs to breathe in fresh air for a few days. A new input of fresh oxygen and Globus will feel as good as new.

A DIRTY FUTURE

Scientists in America have measured how dirty the air is. In 1970, for example, 214 million tons of aerosol spray and poisonous gases got into the air! Among them were one million tons of carbon monoxide, 33 million tons of sulphur dioxide, 32 million tons of hydrocarbon, 28 million tons of dust particles and 20 million tons of nitrous oxide. How can anyone stay healthy with so much junk in the air?

Man has been destroying the Earth's great forests for hundreds of years, and using up many precious natural resources and not replacing them. The use of aerosol cans and pressurised sprays, which contain harmful CFCs, and some chemicals and gases, damages and destroys the ozone layer. This layer protects us from the sun's dangerous ultra-violet rays and keeps the Earth's temperature under control.

Damage to the ozone layer is making our planet hotter and hotter, so changing the environment. This is called **global warming**. However in the last few years, international governments have met to discuss how to stop destroying our planet. We can do something about it!

Environmental Rescue

A breath of fresh air

People in towns suffer more from polluted air than people in the countryside. Scientists have told us what we can do and it is time that we started to do something. Together, individuals and governments can make sure that the air we breathe gets better, even in the towns where there is the worst pollution.

This is what the scientists recommend:

● A good public transport system. If there are train and bus services, people don't need to use their cars so much. Fewer cars mean less noise and less air pollution.

● Changes in the way some industries produce things. They could use less harmful materials.

● Filters on all chimneys to clean the smoke before it gets into the atmosphere.

● Closing down old industrial plants which can't be changed. Some are so old that they cannot be made cleaner or healthier.

● We can switch to fuel which makes less pollution. In the 1970s, when people changed from coal gas to natural gas, the air quality got much better.

● Building big industries outside cities and making their chimneys very tall. This would make the air in cities better. But it only shifts the problem to another area!

The story of London's smog has taught us how important it is to change our habits. In less than 15 years the air was only half as dirty as before. Worth the effort, wasn't it?

It is possible to make our towns much cleaner places in the future. Clean air can be encouraged by the government and individuals can help by using public transport and decreasing car pollution.

Pollution makes you sick

Poisonous air in your body is dangerous. It also makes your body's immune system weak so that it cannot fight dangerous bacteria and viruses. You may catch a cold or flu more easily just because the air you breathe is dirty!

Some serious diseases have become very common in the last few years:

Chronic bronchitis – You probably know that bronchitis is a bad sort of cough. If it never quite goes away, it is called **chronic**. Someone with chronic bronchitis coughs an awful lot, and usually coughs up some **phlegm** as well. Phlegm is a mucous material which is released from the walls of the main airways in the lungs.

People get bronchitis from polluted air and cigarette smoke. When they breathe in bad air, the bronchi become inflamed and can no longer work properly.

Pseudo-croup – Air pollution makes the mucous lining of the windpipe swell up. It may become so swollen that the person can't breathe. If it becomes serious they may suffocate and die.

Neurodermatitis – More and more children suffer from this disease. They itch really badly, their skin turns red and flakes off. Every time they eat certain foods they get a bad rash. So they also have to be careful about what they eat.

Cancer – Pollution is to blame for many types of cancer. Some poisons, such as soot and tar, can cause lung cancer. Skin cancer is one of the most common forms of cancer and is caused by too much exposure to sunlight. Most of the sun's harmful ultra-violet rays are absorbed by the ozone layer but pollution has made a hole in it. This means an increased risk to our health.

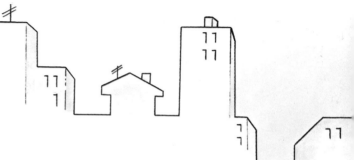

These two guys show very clearly that they don't care about other people. They are racing through town at a dangerous speed. The exhaust fumes from their sports car get up our little friend's nose. He has to cough but the two show-offs don't care. They don't even care about their own health – can you see the cigarettes in their mouths?

HEAVY LOAD

COUGH

COUGH

ACTION AT HOME

Being friendly to the environment

We cannot leave it to the government alone to protect our environment. There are many things we can do, starting at home.

● Think about the raw materials you use every day. Glass is a material which can be re-used. You can return empty bottles or jars to have them refilled (particularly body-care and cosmetics bottles). If you cannot return your bottles, then you should take them to the bottle bank.

● Collect other materials for re-use – used paper, old clothes, worn-out shoes, aluminium and tin cans, batteries and plastic can all be recycled. Re-using materials means that less raw material has to be taken from the earth.

● You can help save another raw material – energy! Don't leave windows and doors wide open when the room is heated, and turn the radiator off when it is hot enough. Take a shower instead of a bath – it uses up less hot water. Do not leave the taps running when you do not need water.

● When you leave your room, make sure you switch off your light, your television or hi-fi set and everything else that is not needed. Don't leave the fridge door wide open in the kitchen.

● When your parents buy something new for the home, they can look out for things which save energy, like energy-saving light bulbs.

● When you go shopping with your parents, help them choose products which are environmentally friendly (they often have a green label on the package).

Do not buy goods which are wrapped up in many layers – a lot of packaging is unnecessary. Take a shopping bag with you when you go shopping or at least an old carrier bag – don't use a new carrier bag each time, you don't need one.

● Make sure that all household cleaning materials are environmentally friendly and do not contain CFCs.

See how much you can do to help keep our world clean and pleasant. You can start in your own room – make sure everything is always neat and tidy. Help your parents by cleaning your room regularly. Put all your dirty clothes into a basket. Where there is no dirt, bacteria cannot live and breed.

If you leave all your things lying around in your room, they collect dust or microscopic bacteria. Dust can act as an irritant and may get into your lungs and make you cough or sneeze. You may get allergies, too. It's best if you tidy all your toys and clothes away. You can do your own cleaning, you know!

KEY WORDS

Acid rain – rain water which is more acidic than usual because it has mixed with sulphur dioxide. Plants are killed and buildings are eroded by acid rain.

Aerosols – pressurised cans with which you spray, for example, hairspray or deodorant.

Allergies – what you have when part of your body, such as your skin or eyes, swells up or becomes itchy when you come across a certain substance.

Atmosphere – the layer of air around planet Earth.

Biosphere – the areas on Earth where life exists – on land, in the air and water.

CFCs – harmful gases that are found in aerosol cans, some plastics, refrigerators and spray action pumps. CFCs are causing a hole in the ozone layer.

Chronic – never goes away.

Greenhouse effect – the trapping of the sun's rays in the atmosphere by a polluted layer of carbon dioxide which warms up the temperature of the Earth and could lead to changes in climate.

Global warming – a change in the world's climate. The Earth is becoming hotter due to an ever increasing build up of carbon dioxide in the Earth's atmosphere known as the Greenhouse effect.

Insecticide – a chemical for killing insects.

Lysosomes – cleaners of the cells. They destroy bacteria.

Ozone layer – a layer of gas found in the upper atmosphere where it absorbs most of the sun's harmful ultra-violet rays.

Polluted – air that is made so dirty that it becomes dangerous to breathe.

Refinery – a place where unrefined oil or raw sugar is cleaned.

HOW MY BODY WORKS

HOW MY BODY WORKS is an educational series that builds into a complete encyclopedia of the human body. Each volume introduces and explains one of its mysteries.

In Part 23 of How My Body Works, you've discovered pollution in our environment and how we can stop it.

PART 24 looks at the immune system and how vaccinations fight bacteria.

READ ALL ABOUT:
● **Different immune armies** which recognise bacteria and fight them.
● **An epidemic of smallpox** and how scientists have stopped it .
● **How toxins invade your body** and lymphocytes defend it.

Albert Barillé, (pictured left) is the author of this fascinating series of books. The human body is a series of complex systems and mechanisms, so to make it easier for you to understand how the body works, Barillé created The Professor, Captain Courageous, Globus, Toxicus and Virulus, plus many other colourful cartoon characters, to show you around. The Professor and his friends guide you through the body, explaining how it works in a clear and simple way that makes it fun.

TEST YOUR KNOWLEDGE

The Environment Quiz

More than one answer may be correct

1. When did pollution start?
a) many hundreds of years ago
b) when the car was invented
c) about ten years ago

2. What is a biosphere?
a) a beautiful place in nature
b) a science lesson at school
c) the areas where life on Earth can exist

3. What is fresh air made of?
a) only oxygen
b) nitrogen, oxygen, argon, carbon dioxide and some other gases
c) nitrogen, oxygen and air freshener

4. Why is burning coal bad for the air?
a) it makes the air too warm
b) it makes the air dirty
c) it makes the air thin

5. How much air do you breathe every day?
a) about ten litres
b) about 12,000 litres
c) about 500,000 litres

6. What do the little hairs in your nose do for you?
a) they tickle me
b) they filter the air I breathe
c) they help me breathe out

7. Where does oxygen meet haemoglobin?
a) in the stomach
b) in the bronchi
c) in the lungs

8. What does carbon monoxide do in your body?
a) it stops haemoglobin from carrying oxygen
b) it ties itself to the haemoglobin
c) it eats up poisonous invaders

9. Why is the hole in the ozone layer dangerous?
a) all the oxygen can escape through it
b) dangerous sun rays may come through and harm us
c) aeroplanes may fall through the hole

10. What is chronic bronchitis?
a) a dangerous type of cough which does not go away
b) an extra long tube in the lung
c) the ending of each bronchi

11. What can you do with an empty bottle?
a) return it to have it refilled
b) take it to a bottle bank
c) smash it and throw the glass into the street

ANSWERS to the **'How My Body Works'** Environment quiz in issue 24.

Answer to issue 22:
1 (a), 2 (b), 3 (b), 4 (c), 5 (a & c), 6 (a), 7 (c), 8 (a), 9 (c), 10 (b), 11 (a & c), 12 (c)

Published by
ORBIS PUBLISHING,
Griffin House,
161 Hammersmith Road,
London W6 8SD

BACK ISSUES
Back issues can be obtained by placing an order with your newsagent or, in case of difficulty, from our back numbers department. All cheques/postal orders should be made payable to Orbis Publishing Ltd.

BACK ISSUE CHARGES
Volume 1:
UK: 99p plus £1.00 p&p;
Eire: IR£0.99 plus £1.00 p&p
Thereafter:
UK: £2.99 plus 50p p&p;
Eire: IR£3.50 plus 50p p&p

**ADDRESS FOR
BACK ISSUES:**
Orbis Publishing Ltd, Unit 10, Wheel Lane Business Park, Wheel Lane, Westfield, Hastings, East Sussex, TN35 4SG. Tel: 0424 755755

BACK ISSUES OVERSEAS
Please place requests for copies of back issues with your newsagent or, in case of difficulty, please write to the relevant address given:

Australia
Gordon and Gotch Ltd, PO Box 290, Burwood VIC 3125 (Enclose cover price plus $1 p&h per issue)

New Zealand
Gordon and Gotch (NZ) Ltd, PO Box 584, Auckland.

South Africa
Back issues Dept
Republican News Agency
PO Box 16034
Doornfontien 2028

Malta & Singapore
Back issues will be available at cover price from your news agency.

© Procidis Albert Barillé
© 1993 Orbis Publishing Ltd, London
N23 93 07 22
Printed in Italy
by Officine Grafiche
De Agostini, Novara